PROSPER

Surviving My Life's Journey

By
Yetta E. Patterson

CONTENTS

DEDICATION 5

GROWING UP 7

BEING BULLIED IN SCHOOL 15

SADNESS OF THE HEART 23

STRUGGLE THROUGH COLLEGE 33

THINKING BACK THROUGH IT ALL 45

WHERE ARE YOU, CYMONE? 89

WANTING BETTER ... SO STOP MAKING EXCUSES ... 107

WHEN THE ROAD IS ROUGH 117

DEDICATION

I would like to dedicate this book to my three kids: Willie Patterson, Jr., Cymone Iola Thompson, and Cassidie Shamar Patterson. I want the three of you to know that as your mother, I've been through a lot in my life, but I've never given up. There were times I wanted to, but I kept praying, and praying. Most of all I trusted God. If it had not been for God, I wouldn't have made it. I've never been on drugs. I've never drunk alcohol, but all that I've experienced in my life might easily lead a person to do so. I just want you to never give up on your life. Your life is what you make of it. God wants us to prosper, but He never said the road would be easy. All it takes is faith the size a mustard seed. I'm asking you as your mother to never settle for less, always strive for the best, and please keep God in your life. You cannot succeed without God. There's no way but the right, honest, and truthful way. I love each of you dearly, always.

GROWING UP

I grew up in Century, Florida. I was raised by my amazing grandparents, who raised me from a baby. My mother didn't want me and didn't like the sight of me, but she did what she had to at the time by not keeping me. I suppose she felt that way because of the hurt and pain she endured during a bad relationship; but my grandparents stepped in and took care of me as though I was one of their own kids. Growing up without my mother was a deep pain I always felt in my heart. I wanted her to love me as she did my brother, but her love was with him. My brother and I have different fathers.

I was originally born in New York, and I would sometimes go to New York with my grandmother to visit. On those visits, my aunts in New York treated me better than my mother, when I was there. My three aunts and my mother are sisters, but my aunts treated me like their own child. My mother used to get mad. She didn't want anyone to love me or care for me. It caused so much pain and my heart used to ache. I cried a lot.

When I was fifteen, I started growing facial hair on my face, and my mother hated that. (I was still a beautiful young lady with or without the facial hair.) She used to say that I was an embarrassment. As I said, I cried a lot, but God sustained me through it all. I love my mother, but she didn't love me.

Being around my family was so amazing, because I felt that I could do anything. My family in New York were go-getters. I had family members who worked hard, and they got what they wanted. My aunts were strong black women. My mother was also strong minded, and I always loved that about all of them. I knew that I was also strong minded.

As a young girl I prayed a lot. I used to always ask God to help me. I didn't know the right way to pray; but I knew if I said those particular words, God would hear me.

Journal the Lesson & Direction

Journal the Lesson & Direction

Journal the Lesson & Direction

Yetta E. Patterson

Journal the Lesson & Direction

Journal the Lesson & Direction

Journal the Lesson & Direction

BEING BULLIED IN SCHOOL

I love New York, but I was raised in Century, Florida. Wow! It was so different from New York, a very slow environment. Living in Century, I had some good times and bad times, especially attending school. It was so hard. I had to ride the school bus, and other kids on the bus used to pick on me, calling me black and ugly. I hated to get on that school bus in the morning, but even more so in the evenings. I was scared.

The kids bothered me all of the time. At the time I didn't have anyone to talk to, but I prayed to God that they would leave me alone. My first year of elementary school was so hard. I hated the students on that school bus. It seemed as though they were waiting for me to get on the bus every day. It was pure hell. However, once I started on the track team and competing against some of the same students that picked on me, things started to change for me.

I raced against them on the track, and I would run fast. I was the fastest female they ever saw, and I meant every bit of it. I out ran the males and females. I wanted to prove to them that even though they were picking on me every day and making my life hell on that school bus, I was going to kick ass on that track. Yes, I kicked ass. I saw it on their faces. They couldn't even keep up with me at all. Time went by and things started to calm down, each day as I got on the bus. I wasn't so frightened anymore, but they weren't always good days.

The other students started speaking to me, and they didn't bother me as much, but I still felt that some of them didn't like me. I also put in my mind and believed in my heart that I was a wonderful person, no matter what they thought about me. Growing up in Century wasn't so bad. I actually had a good life there. My grandmother and grandfather raised me well.

Journal the Lesson & Direction

Journal the Lesson & Direction

Journal the Lesson & Direction

Journal the Lesson & Direction

Journal the Lesson & Direction

Journal the Lesson & Direction

SADNESS OF THE HEART

A few years later my grandfather passed away. It was a sad time in my life, the first death I'd encountered that was close to me. It took me a long time to face the reality that my dad (grandfather) was gone.

When he first died, I was sad and angry. I didn't understand how he could have left me, and not only me but the entire family. I was wondering how we were going to make it without him. My grandfather, Enoch Ellis, was a true BLACK KING. He took care of his family.

My grandfather's main job was at the Jim Walter Door Factory, and he also had a total of six to eight yards to cut in a week, including the weekends. Most of the time, he worked seven days a week, but no matter what he would still attend church on Sundays. My grandfather would work all day and all night. He was the sole provider for his family.

He made sure we never went without anything, and nowadays it's hard to find a man who has this kind of strength. I'm not saying there aren't any good men out there, but it's hard to find one. My grandfather was a KING. I will always love him, but things were a little rough when he first passed away. However, God was there through all of the rough times.

No matter how hard it got, my grandmother had a lot of strength. My grandmother was a strong black woman. She never had a real full-time job, but back in the day she worked for the white people in the cotton fields. Not only her, but a lot of my family members did back then. Working in the cotton fields meant money to our family and other family members. I remember, being young, when a whole lot of my family members would go and work in the cotton fields. We all would load up on the back of the white man's trucks and head to the fields bright and early. It used to be so hot in those fields. I would go with my grandmother, and sit on the back of the truck or inside, all day until they finished picking cotton. That was the only job she had that brought in a little money to help the family out, but that was so many years ago. She didn't have another job after working in the cotton fields.

So once my grandfather had passed away, she had to figure out how we were going to make it. The owner of our house (a white man), wanted to sell the house and land. He told us we had to move or come up with the money to pay for the house and land, and that was a lot of stress on my grandmother and family. All of this happened right after my grandfather passed away.

My grandmother applied for widow benefits and Social Security. She was approved and started receiving two checks. Plus I had two uncles who stayed in the house and gave her money every week. Each month, my grandmother paid on the house and land, and most of the time her whole check would be gone, but she still paid the entire house and land off. It was all paid for to keep things a float, but it was hard without my grandfather. He was the KING OF ALL KINGS. During that time I missed him so much, but I went on and I made it through High School.

Journal the Lesson & Direction

Journal the Lesson & Direction

Journal the Lesson & Direction

Journal the Lesson & Direction

Journal the Lesson & Direction

Journal the Lesson & Direction

Journal the Lesson & Direction

STRUGGLE THROUGH COLLEGE

I graduated from Century High School in 1986. I was on the A & B honor roll the whole year. No matter what, during the time I was in high school, I worked hard, and prayed to God to bless me. I used to stay up at night time, when everyone else was asleep, and I would pray to God. I prayed for any and everything that I wanted, because I knew that God would give it to me.

I also received a basketball scholarship. I attended Lurleen Burns Wallace State Junior College. I loved the school, but I was scared. Leaving home and meeting new people was frightening to me. I did well in class with my work, but on the court, playing basketball was hard. The other players were way better than me, as a basketball player. I was terrible at it.. I felt like a failure. I was devastated. I couldn't shoot worth anything, the other female players were far better than me. Everything I did on the court was no good. The other players laughed at me, picked at me, and talked about me on the bus back to the college. It was just like being in elementary school, reliving being mistreated, picked on, and being bullied. The male and female basketball players treated me badly, after so many failures on the court.

My roommate even started sleeping with my boyfriend behind my back. I would be in my bedroom, and my boyfriend would be next door, having sex with my roommate. Wow! Thinking about it now, and even writing this, I remember how my heart felt, very heavy inside. I would cry myself to sleep. We both played on a basketball team and we both were roommates, but she was a better basketball player than I was. The more I tried at basketball the worse I got. I decided to quit playing basketball and I gave up the basketball scholarship. Giving up the basketball scholarship made me felt better inside, because after each game, I was so embarrassed. I felt weak, and I felt like a failure. I would worry about what other players were saying about me. I felt the same feeling I had felt when I was in elementary school. I was so stressed out after each game, and I knew I had to make myself happy. I was very sad, stressed out, and unhappy. The pain I was feeling after each game hurt.

Finally, I told my coach, Ricky Knight, that I wanted to let the basketball scholarship go, because I wasn't a good asset for the team. He just said, "Ok." He didn't even try to comfort me or tell me, "Don't give up," but once I walked out of his office, I felt relieved. I took a deep breath, and breathed. My heart felt better, not so heavy anymore. I knew that I did the right thing, because I felt good. It's not that I didn't love basketball, but it was not my true calling. I did well enough in high school to get a basketball scholarship but I failed badly on the court in college.

So I started concentrating on my grades, during the rest of the year to bring them back up, My grades had suffered because I had been travelling and playing basketball, and being stressed after each game didn't help the situation. Once that year was over, I transferred to Faulkner University for one year, and then I transferred to North Carolina A & T University.

I was so excited to go, but I ran into a problem. The school needed a copy of my parents' yearly tax papers. (I wondered why when I attended Lurleen Burns Wallace State Jr. College and Faulkner University I had no problems getting in.) I knew that my grandmother didn't file any taxes and the student counselor said someone had been claiming me on their taxes all these years. So I called home to New York and told my aunts about it, and my aunts told me that my mother (my real mother) was claiming me! I was furious. That woman was filing me on her taxes all these years, but wasn't even taking care of me. She had been getting money for me all my life. She wasn't even sending my grandfather or grandmother any money, and they were the ones who took care of me, all my life, but she was still claiming me on her taxes. I was so mad when I found out.

So I called my real mother and asked her if I could have a copy of the tax forms, and I told her the school needed a copy so I could attend. She got mad with me, and said to me, "I will not give you a copy of my tax papers."

I said to her, "You let your own parents raise your child, and you claimed that child on your tax forms... that is illegal! So, I can have something done about that!"

She was mad as hell with me, but I was mad as hell too, when I found out she was claiming me on her taxes. This woman claimed to be my real mother. Who was she? I didn't even know her. I did know that she was my real mother, but I didn't know who this woman was that birthed me into this world. A woman who could hate her own child. A woman who could not be a mother to her own daughter. All I wanted was a copy of the tax forms, so I could attend college at North Carolina A & T University.

Finally, in the mail I received the papers, but it was too late. The tax forms didn't come on time for me to register, so I wasn't able to attend college that year. My self-esteem was very low. I was so hurt, and all I felt was pain inside. Actually, all my life, through the years, I've hurt badly so badly inside. I only wanted to feel love from my real mother, but she never gave me a chance.

As time went by, I finally went back to college at Faulkner University in Montgomery, Alabama. My grandmother helped me and supported me. I just wanted to make her proud of me, but I didn't finish college, because it was so expensive, and it was hard on my grandmother. The only help I had was from my grandmother and a little financial aid, but it wasn't enough, but not once did my real mother try to help me. There were times, when I was in the college dorm, I was so hungry that I would eat Saltine crackers, just to make it through. I had some hard times, good times, and bad times, but God was with me through it all, even when I didn't have any one.

I always wished that my real mother could have been there for me. I always wanted her to be a part of my life. But all in all, God gave me a mother and a father that cared for me, my grandparents who took me in as their own child.

I don't know where I would be without the love and grace of God. I could have been in the streets, on drugs, homeless, with nowhere to go. God gave me a life and parents to take care of me. Both of my grandparents have passed away. Losing them has been so hard and stressful for me. I know that they are in a good place. No more suffering, pain, unhappiness, struggling, and cruelty from people in this world. I'm so thankful that God blessed me to have them as my parents. I always said, if God blessed me to have kids, that I would never treat them the way that my real mother treated me. And yes, I was blessed to have three kids, two boys and one girl. It hasn't been easy being a single parent. There was no help from my ex-husband, only help that has been with me from God. Yes, I once was married.

Journal the Lesson & Direction

Journal the Lesson & Direction

Journal the Lesson & Direction

Journal the Lesson & Direction

Journal the Lesson & Direction

Journal the Lesson & Direction

Journal the Lesson & Direction

THINKING BACK THROUGH IT ALL

My ex-husband only wanted the streets, women, and drugs, I was blind. I couldn't see. I let things go on for so long, trying to love someone who didn't love me. I tried so hard to make my marriage work, but it wasn't the right man or marriage for me. In the beginning when I first met my ex-husband, wow! He was the most nice and caring person. He would buy me roses. I felt so special and I knew that he was a good man who wanted me to be a part of his life. He would take me out to dinner and would treat me like a princess. We were together for about two months, then he wanted me to meet his mother and the rest of his family. I was nervous about that. I wanted to tell him it was too soon for that, but I didn't say anything. I just didn't. To go meet them, that was a big step.

The day came for me to meet his family. He picked me up from my apartment. I was so scared and nervous. I didn't think they would like me or might see the hair on my face and pick at me or say that I was ugly. So many things went through my mind. From the time we left my apartment to when we actually appeared at his family house, I was completely stressed out, but I smiled and took a deep breath. The meeting of his family went OK. His mother was so nice, and friendly. I was so glad that it went well, because I was torn up being stressed about it.

Afterward, so many weeks went by, and being with him really felt good. I really loved being around him. I loved talking to him and just spending time with him. So Valentine's Day was coming up, but I didn't think twice about that day, because I'd never received anything on that day before from anyone. My boyfriend gave me a dozen roses and a ring. I was speechless, I couldn't believe he would give me a ring, and he asked me to marry him. Tears were falling from my eyes,

I was so happy, but I wondered, is he for real, this man who wanted me to be his wife. So I asked him, "Are you sure that you want me to be your wife?", and he said yes.

I said to him, "You make me feel so happy inside and treat me oh so well," and I said yes.

The feeling I had inside was amazing. I felt so happy and blessed. I felt safe when I was with him. He was my best friend. I could talk to him about anything.

However, I knew that by saying yes to his proposal, I would have to let him meet my family. I was back to being stressed again. At the time my grandmother was the only parent I had, my grandfather already had passed away, but there were other family members living with my grandmother. I didn't know how it would play out with them meeting this man that I was with. So I procrastinated. I kept putting it off. My boyfriend kept asking me when he would get a chance to meet my family, but I waited for about five months after he proposed to me, before I took him to Florida to meet my family. On my way to Florida, I was completely a total wreck, but I never let him see it in me. I kept a smile on my face and treated him the same as always, but my Heavenly Father was with me all the way. I thought I was going to lose it.

Once we got to my grandmother's house, I introduced him to everyone, and he just jumped right in as though he was already family. I was so relieved. He told my grandmother that he wanted to marry me, and she said, "Okay, but you better take good care of her."

My uncles really liked him. They started talking about hunting and going fishing. The conversation between him and my uncles went well. The trip was a success and I was glad that it was over with, and I was relieved that my family liked my boyfriend.

After nine months into this relationship, I started noticing different things in him. My boyfriend was mean. If you looked at him, he would say mean things to you. For example, when we were in public and someone ever looked over at us, not really staring, he would say, "What the f-- you are staring at?"

I thought to myself, "Why are you acting like that toward other people?" It was unbelievable that someone could be so cruel to other people for no reason. I didn't know what to think. I felt like I didn't know this man. In my heart I was thinking, "What have I gotten myself into, being with this man, who is so rude to other people for no reason?"

It went on for so long, then he started being absent. I wouldn't see him for days. When I did see him, he would say that he been working long hours at work, but when I called him, he wouldn't even answer his phone, so I knew that he was lying.

During that time, I had a three-bedroom apartment, but my roommates were terrible financially. I liked them, we got along well, but when the bills were due, they were always short with their part of the rent and electricity. We split the bills into three, but when they were short I had to pay the rest of the bills. A lot of times it was hard, but they didn't care. So eventually, my boyfriend told me to let the apartment go and move in with him.

I thought that would help me a lot. I wouldn't have to pay all of the bills by myself, but on the other hand it wasn't a good idea for a woman and man to just live together. I didn't want to leave my roommates, but I knew that I was so easy going and my roommates were taking advantage of me. Every month they were late with their bills, and I was tired of picking up the slack. So I had a meeting with my roommates and explained to them that I was engaged, and that I was moving out. My two roommates understood; they seemed happy for my engagement. I didn't care if they understood. The apartment was in my name and the electricity. I didn't mind that they wanted to stay in the apartment, but they had to pay the bills. Eventually, the two of them moved out of the apartment, after I had left.

Once I moved in with my boyfriend things were good. We got along real well, but I moved in with him, his mother and the rest of the family. I didn't realize that so many people stayed in that house. It was terrible. After two months had passed, I regretted leaving my apartment. I should never have left; living with all these people was hell. When I would buy food, the next day, most of it was gone. I got so tired of spending money for food. His family didn't care whose food it was, they would eat and eat until it was all gone. They didn't care whether I had food or not. Sometimes I would be buying food three times a week. Most of his family members weren't even working.

A total of ten people lived in that one house. Their house only had three bedrooms. Some of my boyfriend's relatives slept on the floor. His mom worked so hard trying to take care of these grown men, and she had two daughters who also stayed there with their kids. Things got so bad with me living in the same house with my boyfriend and his family.

I found out that my boyfriend was selling drugs, and his brother was too. His brother was also using drugs real bad. His nephews also started selling drugs. It was so bad.

One day I was inside the house getting dressed for work, and once I finished I went looking for my boyfriend, so he could drop me off at work. So I went outside, and there was a yard full of guys in his mother's yard. I went to the side of the house, and he was smoking marijuana. I was devastated. I didn't know what to do or to say. I've never been around someone who used drugs, and the idea that the man I was in loved with was on drugs horrified me. My heart felt like a needle had stuck deep into it. The needle just dug deeper and deeper until my heart wouldn't pump anymore. I was torn apart. I cried so hard my eyes were so red.

He had the audacity to tell me that he didn't smoke marijuana all of the time, just sometimes, but later I found out that he also was on crack cocaine. I knew then that I was in a bad relationship. I'm the type of woman who doesn't drink alcohol and I don't use drugs at all. I just don't care for the idea of even having anyone in my life that is on drugs. It's ok to drink alcohol but not be a fool with it. I knew that being in this relationship was getting bad.

My boyfriend stopped going to work. He would stay out all night and sometimes wouldn't even come home. So I started getting sick. A lot of time, I would get up to get dress for work, and would be so sick to my stomach. I thought it was due to being worried. I got to the point where I started worrying a lot, but then unfortunately, I found out I was pregnant. When I went to the doctor, I was five weeks pregnant. I was so afraid. I didn't know how I was going to take care of this baby, because I knew that my boyfriend was on drugs and in the street. The situation had gotten so stressful for me.

My boyfriend was selling drugs like crazy. He had other crack heads, selling drugs to people on the street for him. I tried so hard to talk to him. I begged and asked him to stop but he didn't pay me any attention. The police would arrest the guys that he had selling the drugs for him. Back then it was the 21 Jump Squad. The police would be jumping out of a black SUV truck, which was unmarked, and would arrest so many people on National and April streets. In those days National and April streets were the drug streets; they were hot back then. For the life of me I didn't understand how men and women could be on those streets buying and selling drugs. All they thought about day after day was drugs, and who got jumped by 21 Jump Squad. The drug dealers didn't care and thought it was cool to get caught with drugs. Somehow they would always get out of jail. It was due only to being a snitch or being bailed out by other big-time drug dealers on the streets. I got so tired of the streets. I got so tired of living in that neighborhood with my boyfriend and his family.

As time went by, I got to the point I hated coming home from work. My boyfriend had gotten so controlling. He treated me with no respect. Some days were good, but when he would smoke marijuana or use crack cocaine, he was an entirely different person. It got real crazy when he hung out with his friends at the club. He would stay gone until the next day, while I was at home pregnant and worried about where he was. I would call his cell phone, but he wouldn't answer the phone at all. One time while he was getting ready to go to the club, I asked him, "Why do you always go out with your friends every Friday, Saturday and Sunday and I don't hear from you or see you until the next day?"

He got so mad at me that I figured he was not only with the guys, he must be spending time with another woman. That man got so mad with me, while I was pregnant with our baby. He called me a bitch. The words hurt me to the core. All I could think was that he didn't love me anymore and that he never did. I felt that he didn't want me as his wife and that he didn't want our baby.

The feeling I felt was unbearable. It brought back memories. I started thinking about how my mother didn't love me, and how the man that I trusted never really cared for me either, only what I had. I didn't have much, but he knew that I was a hard-working woman, and when I got paid, he knew that I would share my earnings or whatever I made from my job with him. I suppose you can say I was working taking care of a man.

The time had come for me to have our baby. My baby was born the day after the fourth of July. He was a beautiful baby boy.

When I went into labor, my boyfriend wouldn't even go to the hospital with me. He told his mother to go with me, and he went back to bed. His mother took me to the hospital in her car. I was so mad with him, because he didn't come with me. His mother went with me to the hospital, but she left, because she had to go to work. So I went through all of the pain by myself. I didn't have anyone at the hospital with me. The nurse held my hand through it all. I knew that the man I was in love with, the man that I was having this baby for, didn't give a damn about me. It's not that it was new to me, how he felt about me. I was just trying to be happy, regardless of the bad situation I was in. When I was lying in bed going through all of that pain, I prayed to God to help me through it all. The pain hurt so bad, it was the kind of pain that only a woman would know about. A man will never know that particular pain.

Awe! It was over with. My baby was here. My baby was a beautiful handsome boy. I named him "Willie." Later that day my boyfriend came to the hospital with flowers and balloons, but I really wasn't happy to see him. I never showed how I felt though. Once the baby and I were released in two days from the hospital, I told him how I felt and I told him it wasn't right for him not to be there for me. I went through the birth of having my baby all by myself. The lame excuse he gave me was that he couldn't stand seeing something like that in a labor room, but even if he wasn't in the delivery room, he could have still been nearby the delivery room. So all in all he was full of pure sh-- , and I was so disappointed in him. Days went by and I barely talked to him. I was heartbroken. Yes, he apologized to me, but there was so much: the drugs, calling me a bitch while I was pregnant with the baby, staying out all night until the next day, and disrespecting me for no reason.

Finally, I had enough of it. Two years had passed by and we still weren't married. I decided to leave, and he didn't want me to leave, so he said maybe we should get married. Like a fool, I went down to the court house and we got married. Back then I was so stupid and crazy. I knew I shouldn't have done that. In my heart, I knew I should have walked away, but I thought that things would probably get better. Instead it only got worse.

This man that I married was a complete drug addict. It was so bad for me as a mother trying to take care of my baby and work at the same time. I really didn't have anyone to keep my baby. He wouldn't even keep the baby for me while I tried to work. My husband stayed in the streets, but his sister kept my baby for me a while. I paid her sixty dollars every week for keeping him, but she was half crazy and on drugs too, a pure alcoholic. His sister stayed in the house, but none of them cared whether I had a job or not. I was strong minded, and I kept my job. I refused to be jobless like they were. It was like they wanted me to have nothing in life. It was really a bad environment for me and my baby. I used to be so tired that once I came home from work, I would take a shower and go into the room so I could rest. I didn't get much sleep, because I had to take care of my baby. Once things got settled down, I would be asleep.

Once I felt something strange in my sleep, like someone was watching me. I couldn't wake up, because it was like something was forcing me to stay asleep. I felt like I was struggling in my sleep to wake up, and something like a silent voice in my mind was saying, "Yetta, wake up, wake up."

Finally, I opened my eyes, and there was a shadow in the dark standing up over the bed, looking at me. I didn't know what to think. I said to the figure "Who is that?"

And my husband said, "You know who this is, Yeah, I know you got a nigga in this room."

I said, "What? I don't have nobody in this room, only the baby and he's laying right here beside me. What are you talking about?"

He went on to say, "Yeah, bitch, I'm going to kill you, because you got this nigga in this room. I've seen him leaving out of this room before. I went to get up out of the bed, and he left out of the room."

I didn't know what to think. The next day, I was scared to even see him, but when I got up in the morning, he wasn't even in the house. A few times after that night, in the middle of the night I would wake up and see him standing in the dark. It had gotten to the point I wouldn't get much sleep, but eventually he stopped. It was very scary.

Once I got to work, I couldn't really work, because my mind wasn't on work. I tried so hard to focus on my job, but my mind was so stressed out. All I could do was think about was "What if he had killed me?"

I knew that he was on drugs, and the drugs had him hallucinating. He was seeing stuff that was not true, and not only that, he was verbally abusing me. Day after day when he did come home, he would be looking all in the closets, up under the bed, and saying to me, "I know that nigga is in this house. Bitch, you f---in' that nigga."

The nasty and filthy words that came out of his mouth were so hurtful to me. He talked to me as though I was nothing. I suppose I was nothing in his eyes. No matter how hard I tried to talk to him or tried to help him, he didn't care. He would come in the house and wouldn't even speak to me. He had this strung-out look on his face, and he would stare at me in a delusional way. The look he gave me brought chills to my soul. Once I started feeling like that, I started to fear him.

Several times he pulled in the yard driving a female's car, one belonging to a white lady named Missy. She was known on the streets as a crack head, and she was dating this rich white man. The lady used to come in the hood to buy drugs with her rich boyfriend. For some reason, I wouldn't see the white man that was with her; instead she was always with my husband. I asked him why he was with this white woman, but he would never answer me. A lot of times he would even be in a hotel room with her for two or three days. It got so bad that he would bring this woman inside the house. He didn't care if I was there or not. His family members would be looking at me, and some were even laughing. I thought to myself, All that I've done in this house, and no one even tried to help me or make me understand what was going on. I was so worried and stressed. The man I was married to was a complete stranger. Who was this man that I had said "I do" to? After many weeks, looking at him, as he came and went, in and out of the house with this woman, was destroying me inside.

I finally made up my mind to leave. I didn't care about what I had there. All I needed was my purse and one luggage piece with enough clothes for me and my baby. Before I got ready to leave, I went in the other bedroom, to use the phone, because I needed to close my bank account. While I was on the phone, he heard me talking to the people on the phone. I didn't even realized that he had come into the house. I had my back turned. Once I got off the phone, he was standing right behind me. I went to turn around, and he had a gun pointed directly at my head. He told me that he would kill me. His exact words were, "Bitch, I will kill you. So you called the bank and closed your bank account. So I wouldn't get any more money out of it."

I said, "Yes, I did. It's my bank account." I told him that he didn't even work, or do anything. I had put his name on my account, just in case something were to happen and I couldn't get to the bank, so that he could get money for our needs. He was so mad, but I didn't care. While I was at work before, he had gone to the bank and got money out and didn't even tell me. The only way I knew about the transaction in my bank account is when I went to get money out, and I noticed that some money was missing.

I thought for sure he was going to shoot me with that gun. The whole time I was praying in my mind and telling God, if He let me make it through this situation, me and my baby were going to leave this day. Because sooner or later, my husband was going to harm me, and it might be the death of me, because he was already physically, verbally, and mentally abusing me. It was to the point that my body was tired, my brain couldn't function right for worrying, and I was emotionally drained. I couldn't take it anymore and I was determined that I wouldn't. Once I made up in my mind to leave that day, there was no turning back.

Finally, he put the gun down, out of my face. One of his nephews and his brother told him not to shoot me. He left the house and got in a car. So once he left the house I got my baby. I was already dressed, and I left that house with my purse and one tote bag. I went through a small path through the back yard. I got to the next door neighbor's house. I asked him if he could take me to the bus station. The neighbor seemed as though he didn't want to; he hesitated before he answered me. But I begged him, and he said "Okay." I gave him some gas money, and I got a one-way ticket and I went to Florida to stay with my grandmother.

On the way to Florida, just sitting on the bus, I felt relieved. I felt safe, and I wasn't scared anymore. I knew that if I hadn't left that house, I might not have gotten another chance. I thought about loving someone, when that person did not love me back. Love is supposed to be beautiful, passionate, kind, happy, and gentle, for better or worse, through good times and bad times, till death do you apart. But I knew there was no true love in him for me. I asked myself, so many times, what I did to deserve this. I loved him unconditionally. When he wasn't able to provide for us, I made it my business to be strong and pick up the pieces, but not only did I pick up the pieces, I was the strength in our marriage. I just wasn't strong enough to keep standing.

I wouldn't advise any woman in a physically, verbally, and mentally abusive relationship to stay in it. Yes, I know it's hard, but no woman deserves to be mistreated. A lot of times I wondered what I did. Why did he treat me like that? We as woman always think, we're the reason for the abuse, thinking that we're the ones to blame. To be honest, it's not the fault of the one that is abused, it's the one that's doing the abusing. I knew that I had to find the strength to be strong for myself and my baby. I had worried so much, and I had lost so much weight. But as a woman I wasn't going to give up on my life.

When I got to Florida, to my grandmother's house, I knew that I was safe. I didn't think twice about it. I didn't have much money, only a few pieces of clothes, the ones we had on our back and a few pieces in a tote bag for my baby boy. I also had one bag of Pampers for him. I didn't care, because I knew that my grandmother would help me, and she raised me to be a good person. With all of the stuff I went through, she knew that I did right to leave him.

Once I got settled in, I applied for food stamps, and I was on welfare for six months. Being in the system and on the assistance program was terrible. I prayed and asked God to bless me with a job. I told God if he just blessed me with a job, I would never, as long as I lived, be on welfare and food stamps again. No matter what, no matter how hard it got. Once I got a job, I never went back on welfare. Being the woman that I am now, I don't see how people can be on welfare and get food stamps. I prefer to have a job. A job is so much better than a welfare check and food stamps any day.

The first job I got was in Pensacola, as a long-distance operator at a call center. I loved the job. In the beginning, I was worried about how I was going to get back and forth to work. But when I went to the interview and was hired. I saw another woman at the call center that I knew. We had even gone to the same elementary, middle, and high school. She was a few years older than me. The lady was so nice and gave me a ride to work every day. I was blessed to have seen her at the time, and we were on the same shift. So I was super happy.

I was so thankful that God had blessed me with a job, and I didn't have to stay on welfare anymore. Working as a long-distance operator was an amazing job. I made a lot of money with overtime. We got paid every two weeks. I used to bring home checks, over a thousand dollars after taxes. When I got paid, I also paid my grandmother, because my son was at the house with her, and I gave her money for food and bills. I was so proud of myself for leaving the situation I was in and striving hard to not be in the system on welfare and food stamps anymore. I knew that I was on my way to a better life for me and my baby.

I worked as a long-distance operator for two years. During that time, I started going to George Stone Technical School for Criminal Justice. I received a certificate and graduated so I could become a correction officer. I trained so hard for the training. It was a lot of physical exercise; either it was going to make you or break you, and I wasn't going to let it break me. I finished at the top of the class. I had a 4.0 average in class. I was a straight aim shooter on the shooting field. I loved shooting and holding a nice millimeter gun. I was a good shooter.

Once I graduated I got a job at the Correction Facility. I was so glad to get that job. I was close to home, and I went to work every day. My goals were to work hard, and to get a car and a home for me and my son. Yes, I did get a car. My uncle co-signed with me to get the car. I was glad to have my own transportation. So I decided to go to Montgomery and see my mother-in-law and my husband. A year had gone by before I went back to Montgomery, Alabama.

Once I got to Montgomery, I went to my mother-in-law's house. It was the same old atmosphere. Nothing changed. Her grand kids were all in the streets, selling drugs, and so were her sons, including my husband. He looked so bad. He looked like he was on crack cocaine, which he was. He had lost even more weight. I don't know why I even came back to see them. I just don't even know what I expected. I think deep inside I wanted to show them that I was doing good, that I had worked hard to be a correction officer, and that I was doing better than they were. But what good was that? They didn't care.

My husband seemed as though he was glad to see me and his son. He talked to us, and his mother was glad to see us. She said that she missed us a lot. She even asked when we were coming back to stay.

I told her, "No. We are not coming back to this life." I told her that I was doing well for myself and my son. I also said to her, "Why would you even think I would leave my new job, and come to this life with all of these drugs around me and my son."

I think my mother-in-law didn't give a damn about me and my son, basically she just wanted me to be with her son. I could get him and move him away from her, so she could have peace, because all of them were worrying her. All those grown people living on her was actually killing her with the worry. Yes, she knew that I was a strong woman, but even with me being strong, I couldn't handle the drugs that my husband was on. And I couldn't deal with that type of environment.

While I was there, my husband got my car and washed it for me. But once he got back, I was ready to go. Just being around them made me sad inside. I thought to myself, "How can they let the drugs and streets control them like this?" Yes, I loved my husband, but he love the drugs more than he loved me. To make it in a situation like this, you have to have faith the size of a mustard seed, and a hide as tough as a bear's hide."

So once I left on the way, driving back to Florida, I thought about how badly my husband had treated me in the past, and I knew that I didn't want to be with him. Even when I was there he told me that he loved me, and that he wanted me to come home. All I could see was a lie. I hated to even hear his voice say that he loved me. I thought to myself, such a liar. All you want me to do is work and take care of your sorry crack-cocaine ass, that's all I could hear in his voice. The only thing he was doing everyday was running the streets, smoking and using drugs. He wasn't working anywhere. Yes, all he wanted was someone to work and take care of him. So sad for a man to be so weak but nowadays, a lot of men are sorry, with no job, and they only expect a woman to take care of them. A man is supposed to be the head of his household, his palace, his home. A woman is there to support him and be his backbone.

I knew that I couldn't let his sweet talking get me back in the bad situation I used to be in. I was just glad that I'd grown to be strong and not so weak for him. Once I got back home to Florida, I concentrated on my job at the Correction Facility, and worked hard at being a good correction officer. Having this job, I knew that I could give my grandmother more for keeping my son while I worked. And I knew that I could do so much more for myself and my baby boy. I loved going to work every day, and I was so proud of myself. But being a correction officer is not easy, you have to be tough and not be weak for the type of environment you were surrounded with. I worked in a male correctional facility. Yes, there were a lot of men in that prison.

It makes you wonder, how did this happened? So many men locked up. How did they just give up on their life and fall by the way side? Yes, trouble is easy to get into, but hard as hell to get out of. Being a female correction officer in an all-male correctional facility, anything can happen at a blink of an eye: from masturbation to a massive raid. It was pretty dangerous, but as a female officer, I didn't have any problems at all.

In the beginning, I thought that I would have a problem with the inmates, because all of my life at some point I had a problem with others looking at the hair on my face. So I was obviously frightened when I first started the job. Yes, I'm a woman, but a woman with facial hair. If I were to let it grow, it would be a full beard, but I removed it two or three times a week. The hair would grow so fast. I started growing hair on my face at age twelve. So with my starting the job at the Correctional Facility, I thought for sure the inmates would pick at me, or just give me a hard time. But unfortunately that didn't happen. The inmates respected me a lot. I really didn't have any problems at all. Being a correctional officer the job wasn't bad at all.

Unfortunately, my career as a correction officer ended after one year. I left my job. It's not that I didn't like my job, but I fell weak, while being a correction officer. My weakness was an inmate inside the facility. Yes, I got involved with an inmate. How? Simple! It wasn't hard to do, but that wasn't my intention, because I was a good correction officer. I always said I was a strong woman, but this is one time in my life, I fell by the wayside. I walked away from my job, a job I had worked and trained so hard for, because of an inmate. I just quit my job once that inmate was released from prison. I was in love with him.

I probably shouldn't have quit the job, but I knew that I was bound to get caught. I knew that someone would see him with me and would report me to the facility, if I had stayed working there. Century Florida, where I stayed, was so small. So everybody knew each other. I just couldn't take the chance of being caught, but once I quit the correctional facility, they found out anyway. My name was the talk of the town. I was nothing. I was going with an inmate while he was locked up in prison. I was having sex with an inmate, while he was locked up in prison. I got fired, because I was caught having sex with the inmate. My name was dragged through the mud. My so-called friends talked about me. Not only that, my family talked about me too. Hearing some of the things my family members said really cut me to the core. I didn't have any pride left in my soul, because it was true. Yes, I did quit my job, but I didn't get fired. I quit so I wouldn't get fired and get arrested, because I was a correction officer in the same facility that the inmate came from. Yes, I did have sex with the inmate while he was locked up, but no one knew. I know that was stupid for me to do, but I cared so much for him, and my heart had gotten so consumed in him.

I left Florida with the inmate, Roosevelt. We got along so well together. We were together about seven months, while he was locked up. I moved to Mobile, Alabama, with him. I took my baby boy with me because I wasn't going anywhere without him. Roosevelt cared a lot for my son, Willie, but after so many months had passed by in Mobile, things turned left. We were staying with Roosevelt's sister and other family members stayed there, including his mother. Actually, it was a lot of people staying there.

Not only that, his sister was a big-time drug dealer, plus other people stayed there that helped her sell drugs. Roosevelt's sister had a girlfriend who also stayed there. Oh my God, there I was again, repeating the same life and bad environment I was in, when I left my husband. To make things worse, Roosevelt was a drug addict and crack cocaine user too. I was devastated when I found out. The way I found out was that he would take my car and be gone for two and three days at a time. I didn't know what to think at the time. I would be begging him to bring the car home, because my uncle had co-signed with me to get that car, and the car payment was already behind. I had messed up my uncle's credit. I left town with this man and didn't even tell my uncle. I thought I knew, but really, I had no idea what I was getting myself into. If that wasn't bad enough, I had quit my job for him.

Roosevelt's sister would get on the phone to call him. He would answer the phone calls from her, but he wouldn't answer the phone when I called. So finally they took me to the hotel where he was. His sister had known where he was the whole time, because when I got to the hotel, he was high. His eyes were so glossy looking. He had been using drugs. He couldn't explain anything to me, but I saw it in his eyes. Roosevelt had the same look in his eyes my husband used to have. He was so jittery and jumpy, and his eyes looked like he was high off of something. And the whole time I was asking him why he was staying out all night long and not answering the phone for me, he wouldn't even answer me. He actually looked at me like I was crazy. The only thing I could think was that he was on crack cocaine. I remembered that look so well. My husband had that same look in his eyes, when he used to be on crack cocaine. Once you've been around someone like that, you never forget that look in their eyes. I then got my car keys from him, and his sister gave me money for a hotel room, because they didn't want me there anyway. Actually, they wanted him to leave too, because as they finally told me, Roosevelt had been on drugs all his life.

Once again I was in the same situation with drugs around me. I had no home to go to, no job, no money, and no family members to help me. I had nothing. Roosevelt's sister gave me enough money for three nights in a hotel, but I didn't know what to do. Finally, Roosevelt came to the hotel where I was staying. His mother and sister had brought him there to stay. They were telling him that it was time for him to change, because I had lost my job and given up everything, and for him to get out of prison. After spending so many years locked up, that should have taught him a lesson, but it didn't. He got out and was right back on drugs, real heavy. In a month after serving time in prison, he was back in the streets and on drugs. He was locked up before for drugs and robbery. Being a correction officer, I should have known that, but I didn't know. I was blinded by his lies and deception. I just don't know why I didn't look at his rap sheet. It never crossed my mind. All I wanted was to be treated right and be loved.

The love that I wanted more than anything was the love that I needed from my mother, and looking for love in someone else got me nowhere. I knew then, just like I knew before, this is not the kind of life that my grandmother raised me to have. She raised me well, but despite me being a good person, I kept getting caught up in the wrong situations and environments. So I knew I had to get out of it. Yes, I loved him, but he only loved the streets, women, and drugs. I didn't matter at all to him.

Being a single parent with my baby boy in that type of environment, I knew I had to make a big change in my life. I took the step of trying even harder to get a job. I got one but it didn't pay much. It was a security job. So I stayed there for about six months, and then I found another job that paid more. I still couldn't afford the hotel room fee. I was barely making it trying to pay for a hotel room every day. And Roosevelt wasn't working anywhere. I started getting sick. I went to the doctor. At first I thought it was because of a lot of worry, but unfortunately, I was pregnant again. Yes, by another man, who didn't care anything for me. He only cared about the money I was bringing in.

I found out that I was three months pregnant, but it seemed as though he cared only when he was sober, and not on drugs. No matter how hard I worked, and even though I was pregnant with the baby and had my baby boy with me, Roosevelt didn't care anything about me. He stayed gone all of the time. It would be days before I would see him. When the time came for me to have the baby he was nowhere in sight. He didn't even come to the hospital while I was in labor. He called the hospital and said he was on the way, but he never showed up. The only people I had with me in that delivery room were the doctor, nurses, and my Heavenly Father. If it wasn't for God, I don't know what I would have done. On September 21, 1996, I had a beautiful baby girl named Cymone.

Oh my God, my daughter was so pretty, and my baby son Willie loved his sister. The next day after my daughter was born, Roosevelt showed up at the hospital. I was still there. I stayed in the hospital two days after delivering, but he showed up with a bunch of lies. So I asked him if he could take some money to Rent-a-Center for me to pay on the television I had in my apartment, two weeks prior I had gotten an apartment. So he said that he would drop the money off. He left the hospital in my car, and was supposed to have come back, but he never did. The money was never paid on the television, and he also got shot in the leg and was in an accident in my car. The car was totaled. So, I was without a car. I didn't know how I was going to make it without transportation, but once again God was watching over me. A lady that I had met from my second job came to the hospital to see me, and she brought stuff for my baby. She also took me everywhere I needed to go. She was so nice to me, and to top things off, she was a white lady. Sometimes it takes people who are not your own race, to let you know that they care, and this woman was there for me, and I will never forget her.

After leaving the hospital within four days, the lady took me to a car lot, and God blessed me with a car. At the time I only had one hundred fifty dollars in my purse. I really didn't have enough for the down payment, but God blessed me with the car anyway. I was so happy. Once I got the car, it was such a relief, because I was helpless without one, but my friend was there for me, and I thanked God for her. I drove the car home and there he was, Roosevelt. I was starting to get sick of him. He was lying down, from having been in a bad accident in my car. He told me such a lie that someone was trying to rob him and take the car, but let the truth be told. He tried to take someone's drugs and run, but before he could get out of sight, they shot him in the leg and he made it to the car. He was trying to get away from them with the drugs, and Roosevelt ran into a pole and my car was totaled. So that's the real truth about what happened. I found that out later.

So after so many lies, I had enough. I decided to move back home to Florida with my grandmother, and I had both of my kids with me, Willie and Cymone. I was so blessed and happy to leave Mobile, Alabama. I'd had enough living hotel to hotel, apartment to apartment, trying to have a home with a no-good man, because all he wanted was the streets, women, and drugs. I refused to keep taking my son through that type of life, and I didn't want my newborn baby to go through it. Roosevelt was worse than my husband. I went from a bad marriage to pure hell. The relationship I had with Roosevelt, I wouldn't want any woman on earth to experience. What I experienced was so toxic. The life I had with him at that time was lonely, dark, foggy, scary, and dull. It was a place that no woman should feel in her heart, and a path she shouldn't have to take alone.

I was so happy to be back at home in Florida once again with my grandmother. My heart felt so relieved and my mind wasn't so weary. I knew being back at home was the best place for me. But this time, I still had my job in Mobile, Alabama. So I decided to drive back and forth until I got one closer to home. I didn't have to think about being on welfare because I was determined no matter how hard it got, I would never go back in the system on welfare and food stamps.

I drove to and from Mobile, Alabama for about a month. It was hard, because I was on the graveyard shift. One morning on the way home, I fell asleep while driving, but I woke up in time. My car ran off the road and hit a tree. The car hit the tree on the right fender area, but it wasn't bent too badly. The only thing is that my son and baby daughter were in the car with me, because their aunty and grandmother, Roosevelt's family, wanted to see them. I took the kids with me that night before, so the kids could stay overnight with the family. I picked them up that morning and I was on my way to Florida. I just had got off of work. Driving like that was too hard on me. So I would go look for a job at home and finally was blessed with a new job. Once I got to work in Mobile, I told my manager that I was going to leave my job, because the drive was too far for me, especially after falling asleep, while driving back and forth. I thank God that I and my kids weren't hurt, and I couldn't take the chance that something would happen to us.

My manager hated the idea of me leaving, but he told me if I ever needed a job, I was always welcome to come back. The people I worked with at Central Parking were amazing. I truly loved that job. I knew that I would miss working with everybody at Central Parking, but I also had to make a change for the sake of my life and my kids.

I started working at the gas station at home as a cashier. Actually it was just up the street from my grandmother's house. The job didn't pay a whole lot, only minimum wage, which is still more than welfare. So I was destined not to go down that road again. The job was just fine for me. After six months there, I got a second job working at Masland Carpets. I stayed at the gas station for about a year, only working on weekends. I didn't want to let the job go, because the people I worked for were good people and I really enjoyed the job. The job at Masland Carpets was a full-time job. I was making more money there. So eventually, I stopped working weekends at the gas station. It was too much time away from my kids, and it was tiresome for me.

My job at Masland Carpets was a good job. I loved that job. The company had good benefits and the job was a good source for me to get completely back on my feet. I worked at Masland Carpets for five years and six months. They paid well, but I wanted more for me and my kids. In my mind and heart, I know and believe it's never too late to grow and prosper in life. So my friend that lived in Montgomery, Alabama, told me about a company planning to start hiring, and it would be a good opportunity for me. The name of the company was Hyundai of Alabama. Wow! I thought that would be good for me and my kids, because I wanted more for us. But I also thought about how hard it was before for me to find a good job paying a decent amount of money in Montgomery. I just didn't want to go back to working minimum wage like I did before and I most definitely didn't want to now with two kids.

Also I thought about going back to Montgomery and meeting with that ex-husband of mine, or should I say, my husband. Even though I had a son by him, and it would be good for my son to see his family, I didn't have any idea I would see my husband. I actually thought he was still locked up in prison. Yes, he did get locked up a few years after I first left Montgomery with my son, and sadly to say his mother had passed away.

My mother-in-law was a good woman. She worked so hard trying to make it, but had no help from her kids. My mother-in-law had a total of nine kids, five girls and four boys. All of them were grown and were very responsible, except three of them. One daughter didn't care anything except herself and the streets, just like her two brothers, one which was my husband.

My mother-in-law worked and worked until she was unable to. She was an amazing woman and she loved her kids, but her last three kids gave her hell and the grandkids did too; they never could get their life together, which brought a lot of worry into their mother's life, on top of her being a diabetic. My goodness, I wished I could see her and just let her see my kids.

Once I got an application for Hyundai of Alabama, I filled it out and they called me immediately. I kept my full-time job at Masland Carpets working Monday through Friday and on weekends I would go to training on Saturday at Hyundai. I had to go for five Saturdays. I went and passed all of the test with a 4.0 average, or shall I say, an A. We also had to go through a full floor training, and I passed every obstacle with no problem at all. When the training was over, I prayed to God that if he would just give me the opportunity to get the job, I would do my best, work hard, and give it my all. Yes, God blessed me with the job. I was so happy, it was a feeling that I will never forget. My heart was filled with so much joy.

My family seemed happy for me, but I knew that they didn't want me to leave and move back to Montgomery. I do understand why, because my family knew that I had a hard time before in Montgomery. My grandmother really didn't want me to leave, but I had to do what was best for me and my kids, I really loved my job at Masland Carpets, but I didn't really care anymore about living in Century, Florida. The town was going down, as in run down, with no good-paying jobs. People were moving away, it had lots of drugs, and being home in Century wasn't the same anymore. It was a very small town; you could pass it, without even knowing you had passed through. When I was younger, Century used to be the place to be, but since then it looked so dead looking, and I just didn't want to spend my life there.

God gave me the opportunity to be blessed with a good-paying job with benefits, and I needed it for me and my kids, because I worked hard to get it. When I first got to Montgomery, I had to find a place to stay, so I called my sister-in-law. She was my husband's sister. She let me stay with her. After a month of being in Montgomery and working at Hyundai, I decided to go back to Century and get my two kids. I just couldn't take it any longer, being away from them. My kids are my joy. Going to work every day was good, but my heart wasn't good. I worried a lot about my kids. And I just needed them with me. It's hard being a single parent, but leaving your kids to find a better job and having to be separated from them is the hardest thing for a mother to do.

I went to Florida so I could withdraw my kids from school and bring them to Montgomery to live with me. I could tell that when I was leaving with the kids my grandmother was sad that they were leaving, but there was no way I could be apart from them. Plus I wasn't going to leave my kids on her like that. It would be less of a woman for me to do that. When it comes to my kids, I love being with them.

Once I got my kids back to Montgomery, my husband wanted to see his son, but once he saw my daughter, Cymone, he fell in love with her too. She really liked him a lot and she really grew on him. So the only father she knew was my husband, and he was her father. My daughter never got a chance to get to know her father, because once again, he stayed in and out of jail, and I refused to let her be around him.

Yes, let the truth be told once again. I was back with my husband. We never filed for a divorce. Once I moved back to Montgomery, he wanted me to be with him as his wife; then after not seeing me for nineteen years, plus he never thought that he would see his son. He seemed so sincere; and I never stopped loving him, but I just couldn't be around that type of environment with all the drugs. He seemed to have himself together. He had a good-paying job, plus he wasn't in the streets on drugs. So I thought maybe I would give him another chance, and so that he could help raise his son and get to be with both of the kids.

A few months had passed. By then I had gotten my kids settled in school, plus I was so blessed to have a house to move into. Living in that two-bedroom apartment with my sister-in-law wasn't going to work, plus when she had her grown sons over to the apartment, they would eat up the food that I bought for my own kids. My goodness, it was a sad case. They were some of the same ones who would eat up the food from me when they all used to stay with my mother-in-law. The kind of people who don't care what they do. So I was so glad that I found a house for me and my kids.

It wasn't long after I and the kids moved into the house, a few weeks later, that my husband moved in with us. I felt a little strange being with him after nineteen years, but we were back together again. Once again, things were going so well for us, but it was too good to be true. After about six months, I started hearing rumors that he was sleeping with a woman up the street from where we lived, and that same woman had been to my house, not once, but several times. My daughter Cymone used to play with her kids and a few other kids up the street.

One of the other single parents told me that my husband was sleeping with the woman next door to her. But I didn't believe her. I thought in my mind that it all was a bunch of lies, "he say, she say" stuff. But Lord behold, it was true! My daughter saw her dad, my husband in our back yard, late at night while I was at work.

My husband was in the back yard with a woman. And the back lights were off. So my daughter Cymone saw them, not one time, but several times. My daughter kept trying to tell me, but I didn't believe her. Cymone used to tell me how the lady would come over and her daddy would think that they would be asleep, but Cymone, my daughter wasn't. She told me that she couldn't tell what they were doing, but he would have the lights off back there with that woman in the back yard.

So yes, I asked him and he lied about it, and he even said that Cymone was lying. Plus the lady up the street was lying about him. The whole time I was back with him as his wife, he was cheating on me. I recall one painful moment. I was on graveyard shift (back then Hyundai had only two shifts). We would change only two shifts every three or four months, but during that time, I was on graveyard shift. Once I got off that morning, I had a message on the phone. The message that was on my phone, was one message I hated that I ever got. All I could hear on the message was my husband's voice. He was having sex with another woman. He was telling her how good her pussy was, and telling her to make her pussy calm. It was so loud. I could hear the pressure, while they were grinding when they touched. It was like rough hard sex, bodies hitting together. I could hear the woman screaming in a sexual way and saying "I am calming."

I could hear him say over and over, "Make it calm."

I was hurt. I didn't know what to think. I played it again, and it was his voice, just as plain. Somehow his phone had called me, at the time he was having sex with that woman, and he didn't have any idea that it had recorded the whole thing, and that was the message it left me, him having sex with another woman, cheating on me.

Oh my God, I felt so stupid! The pain I felt hurt me to the core. I felt like I couldn't breathe. I felt helpless, weak, worthless, not good enough and ugly. My spirit was shot to pieces. When I got to the house, he was lying in bed. I thought to myself that I wanted to stab him in his sleep. I thought I should have had a pot full of hot grits and poured it on him. In my mind I thought to myself, "This no good trifling, bitch ass man, laying here in my bed!"

I woke him up. I proceeded to ask him whether he was with another woman last night, and he said hell no. He had a really bad attitude with me, just that quick. I took out my phone, and showed him the time his phone had called me. Since I didn't answer it, the phone went to my voice mail, and left me a message with him having sex with a woman. He actually listened to the message and then looked me in my face and told me that it was a damn lie, and he told me to get out of his face.

He said to me, "And you waking me up with some bull shit like this." So you see, he was already guilty. He couldn't even be calm about it. He went straight into a rage, hollering at me, and calling me crazy.

I said to him, "How can you have the audacity to talk to me like this? Your voice now is the same voice, that is on this phone with your other woman having sex with her."

When I asked him, I wasn't even screaming, but he just didn't know what I was thinking in my mind. I wanted to kill him. So he got out of the bed and got dressed and went to work. When he got off work, I wasn't even home. I was actually walking in the neighborhood, but it was like four blocks over from our house. I just didn't want to be in the same house with him. I couldn't stand looking at him. All I could think about is the sound and the words I heard from the message that was left on my phone. I thought that if I would go for a walk, it would clear my mind.

The more I walked the more rage I felt inside. I started thinking about how much I loved this man, and I asked myself, "I'm not good enough? What is wrong with me?" Yet there I was blaming myself for his infidelity, his sleeping with another woman. I stayed out walking until it started to get dark. No matter how hard it was, I loved him, but I couldn't stand the sight of him. After a week went by, I started to speak to him once I entered the house. At the beginning, I didn't care to speak to him at all, but I eventually started speaking.

Each day I would go to work, but it was so hard. All I could think about was the message that was left on my phone. I heard his voice, and the things he was saying to his other woman, over and over in my head. It got so intense for me, I started crying, and I left work. Once I got home, I started feeling real sick to my stomach and I threw up in the toilet. A few days after that day, I started doing it a lot. So I figured the upset stomach, and nausea came from worrying so much, but no, it came from me being three weeks pregnant. When I went to the doctor and he told me that I was three weeks pregnant, I didn't know what to do. I was shocked. I was happy for the baby, but I wasn't happy for my marriage. All I could think about was my husband cheating on me, and having sex with another woman.

Once my husband had gotten off work, I told him that I had been to the doctor, and I proceeded to tell him that I was three weeks pregnant. He seemed so happy at the time. After I had told him, he pulled out a box and it had a ring and band in it. I was thinking to myself I didn't want it, but I didn't let on to him that I didn't want the rings. I felt in my heart he just bought the wedding rings to cheer me up, and hopefully it would smooth things over with me and him. He knew that he was guilty of it all. So eventually I let it all go and forgave him. The whole time I was pregnant I had some good days.

I worked the whole time I was pregnant. It was hard working on that assembly line being pregnant. Not only that, some of the people I worked with wouldn't even help me. I remember when they had shoulder problems and back problems, I would lift the hood and truck of the car for them so it wouldn't be hard for them. But those same friends really weren't my friends, and they let me know that they weren't going to help me. It was hard, but God took care of it for me.

Things were hard at work but they weren't any better at home. Once I forgave him for cheating on me, he continued to do so. But I didn't find out until my son was born. (Yes, I had another boy, Cassidie.) How I found out he was still cheating was that about eight months later, I was at work and I got a phone call. Amazingly, I was on my break. It was as though the person knew exactly the time I went on break. So I answered the phone. Wow! It was a woman. She told me who she was. She was my husband's girlfriend, and not only that, she told me how my husband also had another woman that was pregnant at the same time I was.

I was so mad, my heart almost jumped out of my chest. So I said to her "Why in the hell are you calling me on my phone?"

She went on to tell me that my husband and she had got into it with each other, and she was calling me to tell me about what was going on. I politely said to her, "Bitch, you didn't call me, when you were f---ing him. So don't call me now," and I hung up the phone.

Lord, Lord, Lord. Right then while I was standing on that assembly line, I asked God to please forgive me because I just cursed this woman out. So I knew I was wrong by saying that to her, but she was more wrong than I was. But I knew that my grandmother didn't raise me to be rude to other people or mistreat anyone. I called her back and apologized to her. I told her that she was having problems with my husband, but I had already left him, way before getting this phone call from her.

All of the times I had forgiven him, but it didn't do any good. I knew he wasn't going to change. So I had to make a final change for myself to make sure that I could be strong for myself and my three kids, and not to keep being weak for a man. As long as a man sees that you are weak, he will never respect you as a woman. When I left my husband, he looked me in my face and told me that I would never have anything in life. I silently said in my mind and heart, "Just watch me!"

So since then, I've been through a lot, so many times I've wanted to give up, but God has told me that he is with me all the way, and I keep saying to myself and for my kids, JUST WATCH ME. No matter how hard it is, I will never give up, because I know I can make it. I'm glad that God blessed me to be strong through it all. During the whole marriage, I realized you can't make someone love you, if he can't see the love that you have for him. As a woman, I had to let it go, because I was dying in my own marriage. I felt that if I hadn't left the marriage, I would have died, and I knew that my three kids needed me. All wanted was to be loved, but I realized I had to learn how to love myself.

Journal the Lesson & Direction

Journal the Lesson & Direction

Journal the Lesson & Direction

Journal the Lesson & Direction

Journal the Lesson & Direction

Journal the Lesson & Direction

Journal the Lesson & Direction

WHERE ARE YOU, CYMONE?

Oh my God, one of the most devastating things that happened was when my life was turned upside down. On May 5, 2016 at 7:20 am, the police knocked on my door. It was so strange, because once I opened the door, all I saw was men dressed in military gear. There were so many of them, they had my house surrounded.

On their uniforms it said U.S. Marshalls. One of them said to me, "Ms. Patterson."

I said "Yes. What have I done?" I thought they were there for me. I was saying in my mind, "Oh boy, I'm going to jail for some tickets."

I was so scared, but they were looking for my daughter Cymone Iola Thompson. So they asked if they could check my house. So I said "Yes, of course." But I knew that Cymone had left my house.

The U.S. Marshalls began to ask me a lot of questions. I answered them and with the truth, because I didn't know where Cymone was. They asked me when was the last time I saw her. So I told them that she came to my house April 22, 2016, and that she had a gun on her. She was very nasty to me. So I knew I had to be careful, because my eight year old son was in the house and he also saw the gun on her. But like always Cymone didn't give a damn. She was so disrespectful to me.

Two days later, she came again to the house and I told Cymone that she could come in the house, but I didn't like guns in my house. Cymone cursed at me and she kept saying to me, "Nobody don't care anything about what you are saying."

So I told her to get out of my house, and Cymone got worse. She cursed at me again, and she started going through the house slamming the doors hard. I knew she wanted to fight me, and probably shoot me. She just didn't care. I told the U.S. Marshalls that I proceeded to call the police. Cymone said to me, "Call the f---ing police. I don't care," and she finally left the house.

By the time the police got there, she was gone, and they checked her room, but I thought to myself, "For what?" because the gun was with Cymone, not in her room.

I told the U.S. Marshalls how Cymone had called me on April 25, 2016, She asked me to put her clothes outside the door. So I did just that. Hours had passed by, but she didn't come and pick the clothes up off the porch. She also asked for her Social Security card. Finally, she texted me on the phone and said, "Your ass is going to burn in hell."

I was so hurt. I didn't respond at all, even though she was rude to me for no reason. I feel that a person will reap they sown. I felt that for my own child to talk to me that way, she didn't love me at all. I also told the U.S. Marshalls that she only got a few of the clothes. She didn't even get the Social Security card. A lot of the clothes were still left on the porch. Two days had gone by, and it started raining. The clothes had gotten wet. So I brought them back inside of the house to wash them for her, but by the time I had left home and went to school to pick up my eight year old son, Cymone had broken into my house and she came through the front window, and got only one bag of clothes, instead of taking all of them. I felt that she was doing stuff to hurt me, but why? I was only trying to tell her what was right and wrong. Since the age of 14, she never listened to me. Cymone was in and out of youth facilities. I've been through so much with her.

I thought that when she got shot in October 2015, that might have taught her a lesson, but it didn't. A guy even ran over her in my yard, but that didn't teach her anything. And before that happened, a guy tried to kill her at the gas station. He had his gun pointed at her face, but that didn't teach her a lesson. She's to the point now, she doesn't care about herself or her life.

So the last time I saw her was April 24, 2016, when she cursed me out. I felt so hurt and my heart was broken. The pain I felt at that moment was devastating. Even now, I still feel the aftershock of that night, thinking about it. One of the officers began to tell me that they were looking for Cymone and that guy was with her (Kiera Nelson) for capital murder. I was so sad then and even now when I think about her.

I love her so much, but my own daughter used to treat me so bad. The only time she had anything to do with me was when I gave her money every two weeks when I got paid, but it wasn't enough for her. She always wanted more, but I had my house bills to pay. She told me that I treated Willie better than her, but Willie always tried to help me, and I treated both kids the same. I love both of them.

Cymone wouldn't do anything to help me. It used to be so filthy, with plates of food left in the room, soda bottles, cans, dirty underwear all over the floor. She wouldn't even wash a dish even when I had worked hard all day. I learned that my daughter Cymone and this guy had taken someone's life. It hurt so bad. Why? How could you have killed someone? Why didn't you walk away? But I don't believe my daughter did it, I really don't. Now as her mother, the U.S. Marshalls had been talking to me every day, but they know that I've been telling them the truth. I just hoped and prayed that my daughter turned herself in.

On Tuesday May 10, 2016, my daughter Cymone and her boyfriend were on WSFA 12 News' Most Wanted for capital murder. When I went to work, it was hard. It wasn't announced on the news until a week later. I made it through work, but once I got home I cried all night until the next day. My eyes were swollen and red, and I had no sleep. I took one day off work, just to think and pull myself together. Working at Hyundai of Alabama, people there can be so cruel and ugly to others. Not all of them are that way, only the messy ones. I was talked about and laughed about by so-called friends, but God has kept me, and he is still keeping me strong. All I wanted was my daughter to make it through this alive. I didn't want her to be killed by the U.S. Marshalls, once they found her. I just wanted her to give herself up. I preferred her to spend the rest of her life behind bars, and I would go visit her, I didn't want to have to prepare a casket for my only daughter.

My heart goes out to the young man that lost his life. I'm sorry for his family, and I truly hate that my daughter was involved in his death. Oh my God, I got so tired of these U.S. Marshalls. They called me every day. Theye asked me, "Do you have any good news for me?" I got so tired of him calling me.

It seems as though, when a black person is involved, the white police officers or any form of law enforcement, automatically assume you are guilty, or lying about something. So many times I wanted to tell those U.S. Marshalls off, but I knew that my grandmother raised me better than that, and I didn't want to do anything to jeopardize my daughter's situation. It made me feel like they didn't believe me. So finally, I started calling him. I wouldn't even give him time to call me. So days went by, and U.S. Marshalls didn't even called me. I called him and said, "Why haven't y'all been doing anything to find my daughter?"

The officer said to me, "Well, Ms. Patterson, we were waiting on you, to see if you heard anything, because we don't have any leads to where they are."

So I knew I had to go to my main source, which is God. I thought to myself, these bastards worried the hell out of me. So it's time that I worry them, until they find my daughter.

On May 26, 2016, my daughter Cymone called me. The call came through on my phone as unavailable. So, I just looked at it while it was ringing. I thought it was a bill collector. The phone rang three times before I finally answered it, and it was Cymone. I was glad to hear from her. She told me that she was sorry about disrespecting me, and she'd been trying to call me, but the guy wouldn't let her call. So they were at the bus station in Atlanta, Georgia. She said that she was in the ladies room. She was trying to get away from him. So she finally got me on the phone and asked me to help her

I told her that I was going to call the U.S. Marshalls. They would be able to help her, and that she needed to tell the truth about everything, in order for them to help her. But once I called the U.S. Marshalls, they weren't able to find them at the bus station. They were too slow getting to the bus station. My daughter and that guy was gone. There was no sign of them in sight, and then I had to go back through the bull shit with the U.S. Marshalls. The officer was questioning me like I was lying. By then, I was really started getting pissed.

Finally, that day I was on my way to work. I called the officer and told him if my daughter was still alive, and she got a chance to call me again, I was going to go and get her myself.

Because it seemed like bull shit that they couldn't get there in time to get her away from this guy that was with her. I was cursing, and I was mad because when I had called the officer, it took him a long time to answer the phone. I had called him four times before he finally answered. I didn't hear anything from her at all on Friday.

So finally, she called me on Saturday May 28, 2016. I was so glad to hear from her again. I had gotten so worried, having bad thoughts and praying that if the U.S. Marshalls got them, they didn't end up shot or killed by the U.S. Marshalls. I was frightened for my daughter. So once she was on the phone again with me, she said she needed her grandmother's address. I said, "What grandmother?"

She said "The one in New York."

I told Cymone that I was not going to give her that woman's address. I said, "Cymone, your grandmother don't even claim me as her daughter, so what makes you think she wants to be bothered with you? Why do you want the address?"

Cymone said, "Because I'm up here in New York."

I said, "What?"

Cymone said, "What is auntie's address, because I've gotten away from him and I don't want him to find me." Cymone told me she was in the Hampstead Park in New York.

I was shocked so I asked her, "How did you get to New York?"

She told me that he brought her up there but she got away from him and ran to the park, and that she needed somewhere to hide from him. I told Cymone, "No, I am going to call the U.S. Marshalls so they can come and get you."

She said "Okay."

I asked if she was by herself and she said yes, and that she asked a guy in the park if she could use his phone to call me and I could hear the guy in the background telling her to tell me where she was at. So I told her, "Please stay right there." I asked her what she was wearing so I could tell the U. S. Marshalls, in order for them to identify her. So I hung up the phone, and I called U.S. Marshalls here in Montgomery.

I told him where she was. The officer acted like it might be hard to get a hold of somebody in the field to reach the U.S. Marshalls in New York. So I said, "You better get ahold of somebody, they've worried me, and didn't even find my daughter."

I found her myself. The U.S. Marshalls didn't even have a lead and he was trying to give me bull. "No!" I told him. "You will get somebody today."

"I guess it's like he didn't have time," I was thinking in my mind, "You bastard, you're going to do something today to help my daughter."

The officer called the U.S. Marshalls in New York. It took a long time, and I thought they weren't going to find her, but thank God they did. I was so happy and my heart felt so relieved. I was so stressed out about this situation because Cymone had called back twice, telling me to tell the police to hurry up, because she didn't want to be in that park when it got dark, and that she was scared. But after 2½ hours had passed,

The U.S. Marshalls called me, and said that they found her. I asked him "Did they found out where the guy was that had her hostage or who she was involved with?"

So the U.S. Marshalls said, they did some back tracking, and they found him too, and locked him up. Cymone swore to me on the phone that she wasn't involved in what happened. She told me she didn't even know what happened, and that she wasn't with the guy at the time, when the crime was committed. All she knew that she was all over the news for capital murder with her boyfriend. Cymone told me, "Mom, I promise, I didn't do any of it."

Wow! I was so glad that the U. S, Marshalls had found my daughter, because my heart was torn. I was so hurt inside. I hated coming home to my house, because it was depressing to me. I hated going to work around the people at Hyundai of Alabama because some of them were talking about me.

No matter what my daughter did, it's not my fault, and I'm not to blame, because I tried my best to raise all three of my kids, and to teach them to love themselves, to love others, and not to harm others. I tried to be the best mother that I could be off of the income I made in order to keep a home for myself and my kids, with no help. Yes, I am a single parent, with no spouse. I've struggled so much trying to make it. I've been homeless. I was homeless for 3½ years, staying with different people, paying them so much money, just to have a home for me and my kids. So-called friends. I remember I used to pay my god sister $1,000 a month for staying at her house and then used to buy food, and she still was complaining about the electricity and cable bill being high. So she wanted still more money. I went through so much. I tried for so long to save some money, but I could hardly save any, trying to pay for staying here and there plus I had to pay court fees and child support for Cymone.

Yes, my own daughter had me in court for being an unfit mother. My daughter left home at age 14, because she wanted to be in the streets, and she even jumped on the Assistant Principal at Johnny Carr School, and she was no longer allowed to attend that school. So I put her in a secondary school, but she wouldn't stay at school. When I dropped her off she left the school and went on joy rides with her friends, and they would drop her off before school was out, so it would look like she was in school all day. So the Assistant Principal at Johnny Carr School filed charges against her. Cymone left home, and started staying in the streets and she moved in with this woman named Eva. The woman was no good. I've gone through so much with my daughter.

It's been so hard for me from 2005 up until 2016, but I've never abandoned my kids. I love all three of my kids, but I wish my mother had loved me like I loved my kids. My mother abandoned me. Sometimes I wished that my mother would show me love, but I know that she never really cared. As a mother myself, I've tried so hard to do for my kids, bring them up right, support them, put them through school, and raise them right. I didn't have any help from their father, but I was determined to work hard and take care of them as best as I could.

My two older kids, Willie and Cymone, have been a handful. When they were younger they used to get along so well, but as young adults now, they have no respect for each other. For all of the things that Cymone has done in the streets, my son Willie calls her a bitch. His own sister curses him out. My two kids are like night and day. The two of them act like they are not siblings. Most of all they don't even act like they are my kids. Both of them drink alcohol and use drugs. As a parent I've never used any drugs and I don't even drink alcohol.

My two kids are still young and I pray to God that they change their life, because I've worried and done enough. I'm to the point now where I'm just tired, and I just want to be free from them. Cymone is 19 years old, and locked up in Montgomery County Jail. My son Willie is 24 years old. He's working at the moment, but once he gets in the streets with those friends of his he acts a real fool, cursing drinking, using drugs, and walking around with a gun on him. Those two kids have no respect for me; they've cursed me out and say profane words to me, but as always been said, "You reap what you sow." The same thing that makes you laugh will make you cry. What goes around will come back around.

When you have parents as a child or an adult, you do not disrespect your parents. So I've prayed and I've given it to God. I can't keep worrying about what my kids do in the streets, only continue to pray for them, because as a mother I still believe in them.

Journal the Lesson & Direction

Journal the Lesson & Direction

Journal the Lesson & Direction

Journal the Lesson & Direction

Journal the Lesson & Direction

Journal the Lesson & Direction

Journal the Lesson & Direction

WANTING BETTER ... SO STOP MAKING EXCUSES

The house that I live in now, God blessed me with this house, because I didn't have any where to stay. I was staying with a friend of mine, her name was Stephanie and she had a mother, but there were other members of the family staying there too. Very over crowded! I and my eight year old son slept on the floor most of the time, but I didn't care. It was better than going to a shelter. And her mother took us in so we wouldn't have to live in a shelter. My older son was living with other people in the streets. He was so uncontrollable. My daughter Cymone at the time was locked up in a detention center in Selma, Alabama.

But things got so bad there staying with other people, I had to move. They were only helping me, because they knew I was free hearted, and I paid my way, no matter where I stayed, but I couldn't save any money, because I was giving all of it away, trying to have somewhere to stay. I've struggled for so long.

My life as a single mother has been so hard. I have three kids, but will always love them. I always wanted to provide a good life for them. I made it through with the grace of God.

I've lived my life, my entire life, paycheck to paycheck, ever since I've begun to work at a job. I just wanted my kids to have the life I'd never had. I don't want them to suffer or be poor, to live in poverty. I want them to have an abundant life.

Lord knows, I've struggled a lot in my life. I've tried to hustle my way through by going to the casino, hoping that I would win a jackpot. Sometimes I did win some money, but most the time I lost. I've even lost my whole paycheck. During tough times were very dark days and struggling days, trying to make ends meet. My bills got behind, and I had no food to live on until the next pay period. I had to go around to different churches and community centers to get assistance food. I used to get bags of canned goods, noodles, and snacks. There was so much food from the churches. It really helped me through until I got my next paycheck. I needed help so badly, and I thought if I could just hit big or hit enough to get me ahead, I and my kids would be alright. But there were times when the more I played the more I lost. I just wanted some money to help me through the situation I was in, but it sucked me under. I've lost so much, but I still made it through.

Like now, I want to have a better life. I work at Hyundai of Alabama, on an assembly line. I'm tired and I'm in a lot of pain. My neck is messed up and so is my shoulder. But the doctors in medical at Hyundai say it's not work related. My wrist is in pain and my right knee, but they say it's not work related. It is, and I'm tired of fighting with them about the situation. The assembly line is so much wear and tear on the body, and I've been there eleven years plus. I thank God for my job, but I don't want to spend the rest of my life there.

I want to prove to myself, that I am destined and I was put on this earth to be blessed, and live an abundant life and to prove to my three kids, Willie, Cymone, and Cassidie, that they can have and live an abundant life, and that they can do anything. All they have to do is trust and believe in God, and have faith the size of a mustard seed.

I don't want my kids to be in the streets anymore, especially Willie and Cymone. I want them to work hard and survive the right way. I want them to know that there's nothing they can't do. Just do it the right way. My son Cassidie, is 8 years old, I have to get off this assembly line, so I can be with him.

We change shifts at Hyundai of Alabama every month. The shifts are 6:30am-2:45pm, 2:30pm-10:45pm, and 10:30pm-6:45am. Every month you have to change shifts, and I want to be at home with my son more, and be in his life, and I don't want his life to be limited. I want him to participate in after-school activities, like sports and other things. The job that I have makes it hard because I don't have any help. But I realized that I did have help all along. God my

Heavenly Father, in the name of the Most High, you were my help. My soul provider.

So I realized that I have to get up and lay the pity party down, stand up and get out of my life. Because I'm 48, but it's never too late. I'm going to keep trying, no matter what. I know that I'm destined to have an abundant and prosperous life, and I truly believe that.

Journal the Lesson & Direction

Journal the Lesson & Direction

Journal the Lesson & Direction

Journal the Lesson & Direction

Journal the Lesson & Direction

Journal the Lesson & Direction

WHEN THE ROAD IS ROUGH

The more I try, the harder it gets. I want so badly to have more for myself and my three kids. I'm so tired of struggling. I've been struggling all my life. I know in my heart that I have the desire to be so much more. I wake up each morning, day by day, hoping and praying for better. I want and need happiness. I want my mind to be stress free of worrying all the time, about making it through each month without struggling. Most of my worry is bills. Each month it's hard for me to even pay my house payment even if it is rent to own. I'm always late for some reason. When I'm late the landlord always shows up at my door and that makes me so mad. He knows that it stresses me out because I don't have anywhere better to live, and this house needs so much work done to it. It was damaged in so many places, even when I first got it. I was desperate, and just took it as it was.

I struggle so badly with trying to get all my bills paid, plus keeping food on the table and trying to do for myself and my kids. I still try to do the best that I can. A lot of times I wonder why it's so hard for me. Father, I need thee. Working a full-time job is not enough for me and my kids. I even have a small business I've been working on for the past 15 years. I have some good days and yet some days I don't make a profit at all. The business consists of 100% uncut body oils. I have some customers that pay faithfully, and yet I have some that are slow about paying me. Yet, why should I complain when I can't even pay my house payment on time? I know I can't complain about someone else doing me right, and yet I'm not doing right.

My intention is to do what's right, but it's hard. I've read and listened to a lot of celebrities, about how they've struggled, been homeless, and yet they never gave up. My heart is so full of hoping and praying for a miracle.

When I'm at work, I look at people around me, and I wonder are there any that are struggling like me. Every day I look at different individuals and my co-workers, they seem so happy at work. I often wonder what's going on in their minds. I wonder how they make it through each day. I wonder if they are struggling to survive, like I am. The struggle is real for me, as a single parent.

I ask God to help me all of the time, and I know that He wants to never let me down. I thank God for the job that I have plus my small business. I am grateful. But I don't want to spend the rest of my life in a factory on an assembly line. It's hard work, and it's hard on an individual's body, depending on the type of process we have to do each day. Since I've been at Hyundai of Alabama, I've worked so many processes during that time. I've also developed a lot of health issues. I have a major throbbing pain on the left side of my neck. The pain is so intense. I'm very restless at night but the company medical department says it's a personal issue. I also have problems with my knee.

My knee has gotten so bad that at times, I have to use a cane to walk. In 2009, I hit my knee on a skid at work, but yet again the medical staff at Hyundai says it's just personal. In all, it's time for me, because I don't want to spend the rest of my life crippled from worrying so many years at this plant. During the years I've put in, I wish I had saved my 401K savings for hard times like this, but each year I had to go in it. Right now, I have less than two thousand dollars in my 401K plan. I'm 48 years old, but I can't let the past stop me from trying.

So many things have happened in my life. No matter how the bad things almost destroyed me, I always reflected on the good things that made me smile. I realize that it's time for me to change my life. The question I asked myself, "Are you living or are you existing?" Well for years I've been existing. My life has been just trying to make it. I knew then, just like I know now, that I want better for myself. I know that I can do so much more. I know that I'm destined to have an abundant life. I don't want to spend the rest of my life in bondage.

It's my time to live and be happy. As I take a deep breath and exhale, just to reflect back for a moment. For so many years, I wondered why my mother, the man I was married to, and my kids have forsaken me. I've poured out my heart to them. So many tears. But I realized that I have to let it go, all of the pain and hurt I've endured. I know that I have to give all of my pain to God. I can't make anybody love me, but one thing is for sure, I don't want to die trying or worrying about it. I pray that one day they will all realize that I truly loved them. Until then or if they will never know, the only love that I want is the LOVE OF GOD.

www.ingramcontent.com/pod-product-compliance
Lightning Source LLC
Chambersburg PA
CBHW021131300426
44113CB00006B/376